Why
are people
Racist?

Cath Senker

HODDER
Wayland

an imprint of Hodder Children's Books

© 2001 White-Thomson Publishing Ltd

Produced for Hodder Wayland by
White-Thomson Publishing Ltd
2/3 St Andrew's Place
Lewes
BN7 1UP

Other titles in this series:
Why are people vegetarian?
Why do people drink alcohol?
Why do people fight wars?
Why do people gamble?
Why do people harm animals?
Why do people join gangs?
Why do people live on the streets?
Why do people smoke?
Why do people take drugs?

Series concept: Alex Woolf
Editor: Philip de Ste. Croix
Cover design: Hodder Children's Books
Inside design: Stonecastle Graphics Ltd
Consultant: Cris Shore
Picture research: Liz Gogerly – Glass Onion
          Pictures
Indexer: Amanda O'Neill

Published in Great Britain in 2001 by Hodder
Wayland, an imprint of Hodder Children's Books

British Library Cataloguing in Publication Data
Senker, Cath
  Why are people racist?
  1.Racism
  I.Title
  305.8

ISBN 0 7502 3716 3

Printed and bound in Italy by
G. Canale & C.S.p.A. Turin

Hodder Children's Books
A division of Hodder Headline Limited
338 Euston Road, London NW1 3BH

The author would like to thank the following for
their help: Alison Brownlie; Michael Cardona; Ruth
Cohen for the case study in Chapter 5; Minority
Rights Group and Christiana Kwarteng for the
case study and picture in Chapter 6; Jill Rutter for
permission to adapt part of *Refugees: A Resource
Book for Primary Schools*, 1998 for the case study
in Chapter 4.

Picture acknowledgements
AKG London 16; Associated Press 22 (Charles
Dharapak), 25 (Eddie Adams), 39; The Bridgeman
Art Library 13; Camera Press 8, 24, 34, 42; Corbis
36 (Sandy Felsenthal); Howard J. Davies 27; Paul
Doyle 4, 45; Robert Harding Picture Library 12;
Hodder Wayland Picture Library 19 (J. Wright), 37
(top) (David Cumming); Panos Pictures (*imprint
page*) (David Reed), 6 (Betty Press), 28 (Betty
Press), 33 (David Reed), 35 (Penny Tweedie);
Popperfoto (*contents*) (bottom), 9 (Adrees Latif,
Reuters), 18 (Rula Halawani, Reuters), 21 (Petr
Josek, Reuters), 23 (Mike Theiler, Reuters), 29
(Mike Theiler, Reuters), 30 (Jerry Lampen, Reuters),
38 (Achim Bieniek, Reuters), 40, 41 (Juda
Ngwenya, Reuters), 43, 44 (Bob Thomas); Still
Pictures 17 (Hartmut Schwarzbach); Topham
Picturepoint (*cover*) (Nancy Richmond/The Image
Works), (*contents*) (top), 5 (Jacksonville Journal
Courier/The Image Works), 7 (Adrian Murrell), 10,
11, 14, 15, 20, 26, 31 (Jeff Greenberg/The Image
Works), 32.

Cover picture: an ethnically mixed group of
teenagers in the United States

Contents

1. What is racism?

What is race?

Some people say that human beings can be divided into separate races. They believe that the various races look different and have different characters: for instance, some are clever, while others are good at sport.

These ideas about race became popular in Europe in the eighteenth and nineteenth centuries. For example, in the nineteenth century, a man named Count Arthur Gobineau wrote that history was a struggle between three races, the yellow, the black and the white. He thought that the white race was superior and would win this struggle. Other writers believed that there were five races, not three. But even in those days, there were people who believed there was only one race: the human race.

> FACT:
> All the differences in skin colour in Europe and Africa are controlled by just six genes out of a total of 30,000 in the human body.

◀ *Schoolchildren at a girls' school in London, England. Children become aware of ideas about race from an early age.*

The science of genetics has now proved that the idea that there are different races of people is false. Skin colour has always been seen as one of the important signs that shows a person's race. The differences in skin colour evolved many thousands of years ago when humans adapted to different climates and environments. But in fact the genetic differences between so-called races – for example, black and white people – are smaller than the differences within one of these groups.

Yet the belief in different races remains powerful. Some people are proud of their skin colour; some people suffer because of it. The idea of race still matters to society even though it is not founded in science. This book will look at why people are racist.

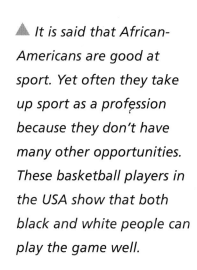

▲ It is said that African-Americans are good at sport. Yet often they take up sport as a profession because they don't have many other opportunities. These basketball players in the USA show that both black and white people can play the game well.

"

'A white child of my acquaintance said to his black schoolmate, "I wish I was black so I could play basketball as well as you." The black child was offended and told his parents about the remark…We often hear this kind of reasoning: "Everyone I see playing basketball is black. Everyone playing basketball must be black. If I am not black, I can't play basketball; if you are black, you must be a basketball player."'
Patricia Williams, Reith Lecturer, 1997

"

What is racism?

When people think badly of a particular group for no just reason, this is called prejudice. To have a prejudice means to pre-judge someone – to make up your mind about a person before you know anything about them. People can be prejudiced against others for various reasons. For example, some people hate beggars on the street because they think they are too lazy to work. Some are prejudiced against people from a different ethnic group, a set of people who share their own common culture, traditions and sometimes language.

If people are prejudiced against a particular group and various things about them, such as their skin colour, ethnic group, religion or culture, this is called racism. People can be racist towards others because of what they think they are like, even if it is not true. Some English people say the Irish are stupid, for example, and make jokes about them. This is an example of prejudice.

▼ *A family at a shelter for homeless people in Florida, USA. Mixed black and white families may suffer from racism, which can make it hard for them to find a job and a home.*

Aboriginal children outside a ruined house. Many Aborigines are so poor that they have to live in tin huts or shacks.

When racism in society is directed towards a group of people, they may be treated worse than others. In Australia, for example, it is hard for Aborigines to get into a good school or to find a decent job. They are more likely to be sent to prison for committing a crime, and for a longer time. This is called discrimination. Aborigines are sometimes discriminated against when they try to find housing. In Alice Springs, Northern Territory, people live in camps instead of proper homes. In one community there are only two water taps for forty people.

In most parts of the world, people do not like to be called racists – it is an insult. Yet racism exists all over the world. The racism of some white people against other groups is a major problem – but non-white peoples can be racist too.

> Article 2: Everyone should have the rights outlined in the Universal Declaration whatever their ethnic group, sex, nationality, religion, political opinion, social group, ability or wealth.
> *The Universal Declaration of Human Rights in simple language, Refugee Council, UK, 1998*

7

What do racists do?

There are different forms of racism and it shows itself in various ways. People may experience:

- People who express racist views
- Name-calling and jokes
- Harassment
- Violence
- Organized racism by political parties
- Institutional racism

Some people with racist views may keep them to themselves. It's not actually illegal to have these views. Others might laugh at racist jokes and pass them on, but they do not really believe they are doing any real harm.

In the classroom, you might hear racist nicknames being used. Some of the people using them might think it's just a bit of fun and that they are not really hurting anyone. But it makes life unpleasant and may be frightening for those who suffer the insults.

Some racists take action against the people they hate. Members of a white family who do not like their Asian neighbours may harass them to try to get them to move house. They may even call the children names, post rubbish through the letterbox or paint rude racist slogans on the walls.

▲ In the 1970s the racist National Front in Britain organized marches through black areas. Here they have destroyed Asian people's shops in East London.

Sometimes violence is used. Racists may take out their hatred on one person they find on the street or attack a hostel where refugees live. For example, in June 2000, three racists in Dessau, Germany murdered Alberto Adriano because he was a 'foreigner'.

In many countries there are racist political organizations that try to gain support for their ideas. The Ku Klux Klan, a racist group formed by white Americans in the nineteenth century, still campaigns today against African-Americans, Koreans and Jews. In the worst cases, racist organizations may get into power and try to kill all the people in the group they hate. This is what happened under the Nazis during the Second World War.

> 'On the night of June 11 three young skinheads drank vast quantities of alcohol, and roamed rowdily through the town's park. They hit the black African, Alberto Adriano, for such a long time and so mercilessly that he died of severe injuries in hospital three days later.'
> Bremer Nachrichten *(adapted)*,
> *23 August 2000*

▼ *Ku Klux Klan members calling for African-American Gary Graham to be executed for murder. Graham claimed he was innocent, but he was executed in June 2000.*

2. Historical reasons for racism

Where does racism come from?

Throughout the history of the ancient and medieval worlds, various kinds of prejudice were common. They were not always based on skin colour; for example, some Roman emperors were black. But people were often prejudiced against foreigners and minority groups who led a different way of life.

People often did not trust visitors from other places, because their customs were different. As few people travelled much, even people from another part of the same country were considered 'foreigners'. And there was certainly dislike or even hatred of people from another land. This prejudice against outsiders is called xenophobia (from the Ancient Greek word meaning 'fear of strangers').

▼ *Romanies leaving Hurtwood Hill in Surrey, England in 1934. They had been living in the settlement for 100 years.*

The Roma, or Gypsies, are travellers. They left India in about the tenth century AD and have moved around the world ever since. Settled people have often distrusted them and blamed them for crime. This has been their excuse to hate and attack them as 'outsiders'.

A racist spraying a Nazi swastika on a wall in Belgrade, Serbia in 1997. There is a lot of anti-Semitism in eastern Europe today.

Throughout history, the Jewish people have suffered terrible racism. When racism is directed against Jews it is called anti-Semitism. In medieval times they were abused and often forced out of their countries. In Europe, Christians saw them as the killers of Christ. At times, such as in fifteenth-century Spain, Christian governments tried to force the Jews to become Christians. They would only accept them if they gave up their religion and culture. Jews sometimes suffered under Muslim rulers. Under Persian rule, from 1507 to 1736, harsh laws were passed against them.

In colonial times, during the eighteenth and nineteenth centuries, these early forms of prejudice turned into a new kind of hatred based on ideas about 'race'.

FACT:
In the Middle Ages, many western European countries passed laws to throw out all Jewish people. Jews were forced out of England in 1290, France in 1394 and Spain in 1492.
A Historical Atlas of the Jewish People, 1992

Colonialism and slavery

Over 400 years ago, powerful European nations sent ships and soldiers to other parts of the world and began to rule over the countries they discovered. This was the beginning of colonialism, and it led to new ideas about 'race'.

The colonists who took over the Caribbean, and North, Central and South America from the seventeenth century onwards needed workers for their farms. They brought millions of Africans as slaves; racist ideas made this trade seem acceptable to them. Africans were seen as no better than animals, or children who needed a firm hand.

FACT:
About 12 million Africans were torn from their homes and taken across the Atlantic Ocean as slaves. More than one in ten died on the way. Those who survived were sold and then forced to work up to eighteen hours a day.
Robin Blackburn, The Making of New World Slavery, *1997*

◀ *A late eighteenth-century painting of slaves in North America. Here they look relaxed, but in fact their lives were extremely hard and they had little free time.*

In some countries, such as South Africa, Europeans took control of the land and made local Africans work for them. Colonists also took over parts of Asia, Africa and South America. Few of them settled there permanently, but their governments ruled the countries as colonies. The Europeans thought the native peoples were not able to govern themselves.

Europeans also settled in places such as Australia, New Zealand and North America. They thought they were better than the native peoples. For example, Native Americans were seen as 'primitive' because they wore animal skins and roamed the land. Some people today still believe that white European people are superior to everyone else.

▼ *A portrait of Olaudah Equiano. In England he joined the campaign against the slave trade.*

case study · case study · case study · cas

In 1756, aged 11, Olaudah Equiano was kidnapped from his village in Nigeria. An African blacksmith took him as a slave. Olaudah had several other African owners before being sent on a slave ship to Barbados in the Caribbean. He was then taken to Virginia, North America and forced to work on a tobacco plantation. A naval captain bought him next, and he spent several years at sea.

In 1766, Equiano bought his freedom. Working as a sailor, he had many adventures. In Italy he saw the volcano Vesuvius erupt, he narrowly escaped being made a slave again in the USA, and was shipwrecked in the Bahamas. Equiano moved to England and in 1789 published his autobiography.

Fascism

In the 1920s and 1930s some countries, such as Italy, Spain and Germany, came under fascist rule. Fascists believed their nation was superior to others. Ruled by a powerful leader or dictator, they discriminated against people from other countries or cultures, and used force to conquer other countries. Fascist governments had the support of the mass of the population who were neither rich nor poor. These were people who felt powerless between the influence of big business on the one hand and the workers in their trade unions on the other hand.

The Nazi government in Germany was the most racist of the fascist powers. Its leader, Adolf Hitler, believed that 'Aryans' – blue-eyed Germans and Scandinavians – were a superior race. Other races, such as the Slavs and Africans, were fit only to be slaves. Worst of all were the Jews; all Germany's problems were blamed on them.

▼ *An elderly Jewish man being stopped by Nazis in Berlin, Germany in 1933.*

14

FACT:
The Jewish population before the Second World War and the approximate numbers killed in eastern European countries:

	Before	Killed
Poland	3,250,000	3,000,000
USSR	2,800,000	1,200,000
Romania	800,000	350,000
Hungary	400,000	300,000
Czechoslovakia	315,000	270,000

A Historical Atlas of the Jewish People, 1992

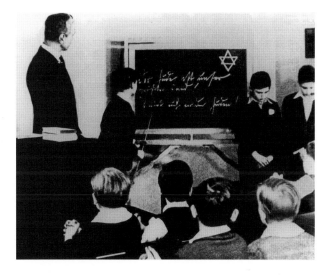

Two Jewish boys being shamed in their classroom in Nazi Germany in the early 1930s. Underneath the Star of David on the board it says 'The Jew is our greatest enemy. Beware of the Jew.'

During the Second World War, the Nazis wanted to kill all the Jews in Europe, down to the very last man, woman and child. In 1941 they built death camps in Poland, where they used poison gas to murder thousands of Jews every day. Millions of other people hated by the Nazis, such as Roma, Poles, Russians, gays and disabled people, also died in these camps.

There was racism in the countries that fought against Hitler, too. A fascist party tried to gain influence in Britain before the Second World War. Racism in the USA meant that black and white people mostly lived separate lives. After the war, many people felt that racism was bad. But the ideas did not die away altogether.

3. The fear of the unknown

How can ignorance spread racism?

When people don't know anything about another country or culture, they may believe nasty ideas that they have heard about it. They build up a picture in their heads about that culture – usually a negative one – and think bad things about all the people who belong to it.

When you think that something is true of a whole group of people, this is a stereotype. People can be stereotyped because of their sex – for example, 'All men are strong' – or their age, 'All children are noisy'. Stereotypes are not based on fact and they are usually insulting. They mean you are not looking at a person as an individual.

Sometimes people are stereotyped because they have a different skin colour, culture or religion. Things may be said about a group of people that are true of only some of them, for instance, 'All Jews are rich'. Most Jews are not rich, so this is an example of a stereotype.

▼ *A poster for an anti-Semitic exhibition in Munich, Germany in 1937. It shows a stereotype of a Jewish person, who is interested only in money.*

Things may be said that are not true at all. White people may hear that Asians eat with their fingers from the same bowl. A few may think this is a filthy, primitive habit, and assume that these must be dirty people. They do not know that picking up food with freshly washed fingers is a perfectly clean way to eat a meal. Possibly it is cleaner than eating with cutlery that was washed in a bowlful of dirty dishes in lukewarm soapy water, and then probably not rinsed!

But those people do not know this – they are ignorant about Asian culture. They believe their own ways are better. Perhaps they then pass on their stereotyped view of 'dirty Asians' to other people. This is how racist ideas can spread.

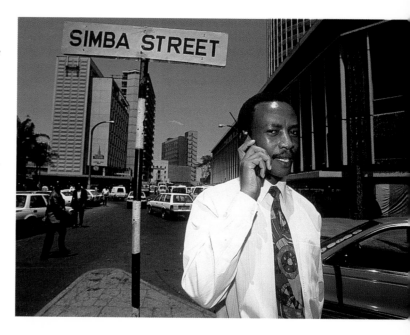

▲ A photo of Nairobi, Kenya, showing the city's modern office blocks and a wealthy Kenyan. It is not true that everyone in African countries is poor and lives in a village.

'During a lesson on Kenya a class was shown a set of slides of Nairobi city centre, with its skyscrapers and modern office blocks. Yet when asked what they noticed, the first thing they mentioned was a beggar, hardly visible, in the corner of one of the slides.'

Angela Grunsell and Ros Wade, 'Multicultural Teaching to Combat Racism in School and Community', 1995

Cultural differences

Sometimes people are racist towards another ethnic group. An ethnic group is a community of people who share the same culture, and often the same language. For example, Chinese-Americans in the USA may speak their own language at home, follow their own customs and eat different types of food from most people around them. Some Americans may say that this group does not fit into their society because they have a foreign way of life.

Racism can often be linked to religion, too. For example, it has been said that Muslim Asians in Western countries suffer from 'double racism'. They are discriminated against because of the colour of their skin, and also because they practise Islam.

▼ *Muslims praying in front of the Dome of the Rock in Jerusalem. The conflict between Israelis and Palestinians is often seen as a cultural and religious battle between Judaism and Islam.*

An American Sikh family in New York, USA. People need to feel that they can dress according to their culture, without fear of being attacked for looking different.

The fear of Islam is really strong in many countries with a Muslim minority, such as the USA, Britain, France and Spain. Stereotypes about Islam are common – for example, that it is a cruel religion. Other myths are that all Muslims are terrorists, or that they are 'mad mullahs' who take their religion to extremes.

Some people do not say out loud that they hate other ethnic groups because it is not acceptable to admit that you are a racist. Instead, they talk about cultural differences. For example, in the 1990s, Jean-Marie Le Pen, leader of the extreme right-wing National Front in France, argued that it is impossible for people from Western and non-Western cultures to live happily together because they are so different.

'At school they would say: "Are you a terrorist?" And I would say "No, I am from Libya" and they would say, "Yes, from Colonel Gaddafi" and I would say "No, from Libya. He is just the president there." '
Sarina, 18, whose parents came to Britain from Libya

We don't trust you

There are Roma communities in the USA, Australia, Turkey and South Africa as well as in Europe. They suffer from racism for various reasons. People are suspicious of them because they prefer to move from place to place rather than living in one spot. They have dark skin, and their own language and culture. Non-Roma travellers also suffer discrimination – even if they are white.

Stereotypes of Roma and travellers are common. They are often forced to camp in filthy places, so people say they are dirty. Some say they are criminals and cannot be trusted.

FACT BOX:
The six largest Roma populations in Europe
Romania	2,100,000
Bulgaria	750,000
Spain	725,000
Hungary	575,000
Slovakia	500,000
Turkey	400,000

Donal Kenrick, An Historical Dictionary of the Gypsy People, quoted by the Refugee Council, 1998

▼ *An elderly Roma couple in Granada, Spain.*

Settled people do not want their children to mix with them. For example, in Bilbao, Spain in 1999, local parents protested when they found out that three Roma children were to come to their children's school. The Roma are rarely welcomed.

▶ *Czech Roma protesting against a wall built to separate them from other people, October 1999.*

case study · case study · case study · case study · case study

Josef is a Roma refugee from Slovakia. His family had homes, cars and money there, but they were forced to flee. In Slovakia, the Roma are blamed for crimes they did not commit. They are attacked by gangs of skinheads, helped by the police. The skinheads wear boots with black laces. If they have beaten up lots of Roma, they wear white laces instead, like a medal.

Josef was attacked one afternoon by a group of skinheads. A week later he saw the leader of the group in police uniform. He went to the police station and told the officers about this, but they did not investigate. Then the police called him in and questioned him about various crimes. They beat him up, too.

Josef fled with his family to the UK in 1997. He now lives in Dover. Life is not easy for them because many people in Dover are racist towards the Roma.

4. Scapegoating leads to racism

What is scapegoating?

Sometimes a group of people is wrongly blamed for causing problems. This is called scapegoating. For instance, asylum seekers may be moved into an area where housing is run down and there are not enough jobs. Some locals think that their situation will get worse because the newcomers will compete with them for housing and jobs. The lack of houses and work are not the asylum seekers' fault. Yet people may develop racist attitudes towards them, and some might even attack them.

When Idi Amin came to power in Uganda in 1971, he scapegoated the Ugandan Asians, an ethnic minority group, for all the country's problems. He said the Asians controlled too much of the economy. Many Africans were willing to believe that the Asians were taking the country's wealth and they were pleased when Amin forced them out in 1972. But after the Asians left, their businesses failed and the economy collapsed.

There are around 25 million ethnic Chinese people living in South-east Asian countries. In some places they have been scapegoated because governments fear they have too much economic power.

▼ *Rioters in Medan in northern Sumatra, Indonesia burning motorcycles stolen from a shop owned by ethnic Chinese people, May 1998.*

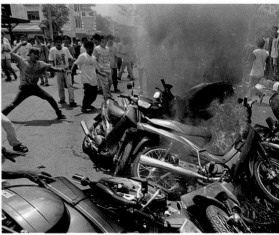

At times of economic and political crisis, racist policies have been directed against them. In the worst cases they have been forced out of the country. In May 1998 the Chinese community was scapegoated for the problems in Indonesia and suffered vicious attacks. At least 2,000 people were killed in the capital Jakarta alone.

People who suffer racism themselves may scapegoat other groups. For example, angered by their poverty and lack of opportunities, African-Americans in the USA have attacked Korean shopkeepers. Louis Farrakhan, leader of the African-American organization the Nation of Islam, believes all whites are evil, and is very anti-Semitic.

> 'Maybe the separation [of the races] might be the best answer.'
> *Louis Farrakhan, March 1997*

▼ *Louis Farrakhan speaking to hundreds of thousands of marchers who came on the One Million Man March to Washington DC, USA in 1995.*

'Keep them out!'

What do you do if you cannot live in your country any more because you are being attacked because of your skin colour, culture, religion or political views? You will probably seek asylum in a nearby country. If you want to go to a country in the European Union, you will find it difficult – even if you are European yourself. Many asylum seekers in the European Union (EU) are victims of the wars in the former USSR and Yugoslavia who have lost their homes and jobs.

Asylum seekers in the European Union are often:
• Separated from the rest of the population
• Placed in hostels
• Not allowed to work
• Given coupons instead of money to buy food (as happens in Germany and Britain)

◀ *A man being arrested after a neo-Nazi attack on a hostel for refugees in Rostock, Germany in 1993. The number of racist attacks in Germany is increasing today.*

These policies can lead to scapegoating. The new arrivals are seen as 'scroungers' getting something for nothing. Throughout the 1990s there were racist attacks on hostels in countries such as Germany, Holland, Sweden and Austria. Often, the racists try to burn down the buildings – sometimes with the people still inside.

▶ *A Vietnamese woman and child fleeing Communist Vietnam on a fishing boat, 1977. Ethnic Chinese people also fled Vietnam by boat to escape racism.*

case study · case study · case study · case study · case study

In 1978, ethnic Chinese people began to leave Vietnam after anti-Chinese racism increased. Most fled to other South-east Asian countries. From 1979 to 1992, small numbers of Vietnamese refugees were allowed to enter Australia, Canada, the USA and Europe.

Quang Bui's brother escaped from Vietnam by boat. It was a dangerous voyage, and many died of thirst or drowned in the rough seas. After a long and difficult journey, Quang Bui's brother reached Sweden and was allowed to settle there as a refugee. Quang Bui and his parents were later able to join him.

When he first arrived, Quang Bui was called 'yellow neck' and other racist names by older Swedish boys. But the Vietnamese kids stood up to them and nowadays everyone mixes together happily.

Racism and the media

The pictures we see in the newspapers and on TV influence the way we view people from other countries and cultures. Perhaps you only see Africans starving in village shacks or fighting wars. You may not know about the millions who live in flats or houses like you and go to work or school each day. This lack of information can lead to stereotyping of other peoples.

For many years, films in the USA presented a stereotyped view of African-Americans, Chinese people and Native Americans. Black people were never shown as important, powerful or clever. The Chinese were portrayed as cruel and not to be trusted, and Native Americans as savages who killed white people.

▼ Spike Lee (left) has made many movies showing the lives of African-Americans. His work has helped to create a new respect for African-American cinema, and has encouraged black actors and directors.

Things are getting better. There are now more black and Hispanic actors in the USA making programmes showing non-white people in a wide range of roles. African-American film director Spike Lee makes movies showing the problems of racism; many people around the world watch them. Publishers of children's books nowadays usually take pains to show people from different ethnic groups and avoid stereotyping.

Yet racism is still sometimes whipped up by the media. In many European countries, newspapers brand asylum seekers as people making 'bogus' asylum claims who are 'flooding' the country. A writer for the *Irish Times* found that in 2000 nearly all the local newspapers in Ireland wrote bad things about the asylum seekers moving into their area. The newcomers are often scapegoated for society's problems such as unemployment. Words written in the papers can encourage attacks on the streets.

▲ *Workers from the Refugee Arrivals Project at Heathrow Airport, England helping asylum seekers. Many asylum seekers arrive alone after a long and difficult journey, and do not speak English.*

"
'German Jews pouring into this country
The way stateless Jews from Germany are pouring into this country is becoming an outrage.'
The Daily Mail, *20 August 1938*

'Why do we let in this army of spongers?
So many asylum seekers are pouring into this country...that the authorities here are finding that they simply can't cope...'
The Daily Mail, *26 September 1998*
"

5. Institutional racism

What is institutional racism?

Institutional racism happens when the way that society is organized, from the job market to the system governing housing and education, means that certain minorities are treated unfairly. It happens even if racism itself is against the law. People from those minorities tend to live in bad housing and get a poor education, which means they are likely to get low-paid jobs when they leave school.

The unequal treatment of African-American and Hispanic people in the USA makes it hard for them to escape from the poverty of inner-city ghettos. Suppose that a Hispanic woman from Pilsen, Chicago, who managed to get a university degree, applies for a good job and is called for interview.

FACT: 41.9 per cent of African-American children live below the poverty line.
Institute for Jewish Policy Research and American Jewish Committee, 1998

Hispanic farm workers who have come to the USA to work. As they are migrants, they have few rights, and they may be thrown out of the country if they try to set up a trade union.

It is hard to escape the effects of institutional racism, but music may offer a chance to Keisha, an African-American living in Chicago. Keisha was born a crack baby (addicted to the drug crack). Her mother left when she was young, and Keisha went to live with her white grandmother. She started learning the viola at school when she was eight. Her grandmother encouraged her.

In 1996, Keisha won a scholarship to the Merit Music Programme, an inner-city music centre. Music became the focus of her life. Although she was thrown out of secondary school because of bad behaviour, she carried on playing the viola. Keisha became one of the best students at Merit. Now 15, she hopes to study music at university.

Her interviewer does not hate Hispanic people, but she feels that someone from Pilsen is unlikely to succeed, and that a Hispanic person may not 'fit in'. The woman is less likely to get the job than a white person. It will be hard for her to raise her family out of the poverty in which they live.

This helps to explain why there are only relatively few successful black businesspeople, politicians and TV stars. One in every three African-American families and one in four Hispanic families is poor.

▶ *In 2001, Colin Powell gained the important job of US Secretary of State.*

'We were here first'

Australia's Cathy Freeman carrying both the Aboriginal and Australian flags after winning the women's 400-metre final at the Sydney Olympic Games in 2000.

Native peoples in some countries face problems because their lands are run by other people who see them as inferior. It is hard for them to find a good home and make a living in their own land. How did this system of racism come about?

It has historical roots. For example, in the nineteenth century, European settlers went to Australia and took land from the Aborigines. At the same time, the Native Americans of North America were removed from their land and forced to live on reservations. In the twentieth century, European settlers in South Africa brought in a system of laws called apartheid (an Afrikaans word meaning 'separation') to discriminate against the native Africans.

The settlers thought this behaviour was acceptable because they viewed the native peoples as 'primitive' and unable to rule themselves. In many countries, this attitude can still be found.

A Maya teacher with students, Guatemala. Since the 1980s many schools have been set up to teach the Maya in their own language.

The native Maya of Guatemala in Central America were almost wiped out by Spanish invaders in the sixteenth century. They have remained at the bottom of Guatemalan society ever since. The Maya own little land in the country that was once theirs, and most live in poverty. In the 1980s at least 20,000 of them were killed by the army during a civil war fought over land and human rights. The Maya still suffer institutional racism because of their low position in society. They are often ignored when they go to government hospitals for treatment. People overcharge them in shops and on buses. They are always being told they are lazy and dirty, and need 'civilizing'.

> 'You can't teach the Indians anything. How many times have we tried to improve their way of life? They just won't change.'
> *Typical comment about the Maya quoted by the Minority Rights Group, UK, 1994*

Racism in education

If you are from a group in society that suffers from institutional racism, how does it affect your school life? To start with, if you live in a run-down area, you are less likely to get into a good school. If you do manage it, you may find there is little understanding of your culture and traditions. Teachers may have stereotyped views that affect how they treat you.

Children from ethnic minority groups often do worse at school. For example, in 1999, David Blunkett, the Secretary of State for Education in the UK, admitted that schools were failing Afro-Caribbean students. White students usually leave school at 16 or 18 with much better qualifications than black students.

As well as institutional racism, open racism is common. Some kids are bullied, or even attacked, at school because of their ethnic group. Muslim girls may be harassed for wearing headscarves and long dresses. Mixed race children may be bullied by both white and black children.

▼ Muslim schoolgirls at Al-Ghazaly school in Jersey City, USA. In some places Muslims have set up their own schools so that their children do not suffer from racism at school.

Although it is rare, there have been cases of white children being attacked in response to attacks on non-whites. In the USA, some white children with African-American friends suffer racist abuse for wearing 'black' fashions and hanging out with black buddies.

In many schools, teachers and students are aware of the problems of racism and try to deal with racist behaviour. It also helps if the school curriculum involves learning about the different cultures in your society, and how to respect them all. This makes each member of the school feel valued.

▶ *Children at Alexandria Park primary school in Zimbabwe, where black and white students are taught together.*

FACT:
In the USA, almost two-thirds of money given to students to help them to go to university in 1998 was in the form of loans – money to be paid back. In general, white students will borrow money to pay to go to a good university, believing they will be able to pay it back when they get a good job. Black students are usually worried about borrowing a lot of money, so they tend to go to lower-grade universities.
Derek Price, sociologist, July 2000

6. Feeling superior

How can nationalism lead to racism?

Are you proud of your country? Many people feel attached to the land where they were born, and are proud of its culture and history – they are nationalists. Extreme nationalists may believe that only people born in their country have a right to live there, and make others feel unwelcome. They believe they are superior to the newcomers.

This feeling is more common if the new arrivals come from a different ethnic group or culture. It can lead to racist attitudes towards them. White immigrants from Australia, New Zealand and South Africa have rarely had problems settling in Europe. Yet Afro-Caribbean, African and Asian immigrants have suffered from racism.

▶ *A crowd waving Stars and Stripes flags in New York, USA. Nationalism can bring people together, but it can also turn them against outsiders.*

Even minority groups who have lived in another country for generations may experience racism. The Koreans are the largest ethnic minority in Japan. They suffer discrimination in housing and jobs, even if they have lived there all their lives. Many Japanese feel superior to the Koreans and also to black immigrants, believing that they simply do not fit into their society.

'Many sangokujin [third-world people] and other foreigners who have entered Japan illegally have repeatedly committed atrocious crimes. In the event of a major earthquake, even riots may break out.'

Tokyo Governor Shintaro Ishihara, 9 April 2000

In fact, most countries are made up of a mixture of different cultures, ethnic groups and religions. But racists tend to believe that their country has only one true culture, for example, the idea of England as a land of cricket on the village green, fish 'n' chips – and no black people. The real reason for these attitudes may be that there are problems in society. It is easy to believe that kicking out 'foreigners' will bring back a happy golden past.

▼ *Workers from the Philippines in Kuwait City, Kuwait. Many Filipinos work as servants in the Gulf States to make money to send home to their families.*

'We're better than you'

If you can't make a good living in your country, you may decide to move abroad. Since the Second World War, there has been mass migration from the poorer to the richer regions of the world.

Immigrants are needed to fill jobs – often the badly paid jobs that no one else wants to do. Some people, when they see the newcomers sweeping the streets or cleaning the toilets, may feel they are superior to them. In this way racist views can start to spread.

FACT:
The percentage of whites in the USA dropped from 75.7 per cent in 1991 to 71.9 per cent in 2000. The population in 2000 was
Whites: 196.1 million
African-Americans:
34.9 million
Hispanics: 31.4 million
Asians: 10.9 million
Native Americans:
2.4 million
US Government Report, 2000

◀ *Mexican food stalls with signs in Spanish and English in San Antonio, Texas, USA. Many people whose families come from Mexico live in San Antonio, so a lot of the shops there sell Mexican food.*

Out of 100 million Mexicans, around 40 million live in poverty. About 7 million of them live in the USA, mostly doing low-paid jobs. Some white Americans feel that Mexican customs, food and the Spanish language – which they believe are inferior to their own – are 'swamping' their country. They find it hard to accept that they live in a nation made up of many cultures. This can lead to anti-Mexican racism.

The US and European economies need well-qualified immigrants, such as computer programmers from India. Yet some people, who believe that immigrants from poor countries are inferior, find it hard to accept the newcomers even though they are highly skilled and valuable to society.

▼ *These computer users in Bangalore, India may one day use their skills working in the USA or Europe.*

case study · case study · case study · case s

Christiana Kwarteng came to the Netherlands from Ghana with her family. Before she arrived, she thought that all Dutch people were blond and friendly. She believed that they spoke German, lived freely and were rich. She thought it would be hard to find work there.

Christiana found that it was indeed hard to find a job. But she saw that only some people had blond hair, and not everyone was friendly. Some people were racist and discriminated against her. Also, young people had little respect for the elderly, which she felt was wrong. All in all, some things were better in the Netherlands, but she didn't find that European ways were superior in all respects.

Fascism rears its ugly head

After the horrors of the Second World War, why are there still fascists today? It seems there will always be some people who feel that their ethnic group is superior to all others. There are fascist organizations around the world, notably in Europe, the USA, South Africa and India.

In some European countries, including Austria, Germany, France, Denmark and Belgium, fascist parties have gained some political power. Their members do not openly say they are racist. Instead they talk about protecting their national culture. They refer to the problem of poverty, and argue that money should be spent on local people whose families have always lived there – they mean white people. This argument appeals to some voters; it is easy to blame immigrants for problems in society that are actually quite complicated.

'As more immigrants bring their children into western Europe, the indigenous population is slowly being substituted by aliens.'

Jörg Haider, Governor of Carinthia, Austria, 1995

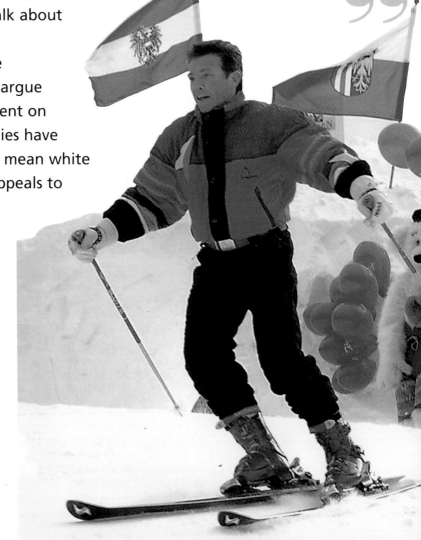

▶ *Jörg Haider, leader of the extreme right Freedom Party in Austria.*

In the USA there are small fascist groups. They do not have political power, but they are active in other ways. They attack African- and Asian-Americans, Jews, Koreans and gay people, set fire to their homes or vandalize their property. Between 1988 and 1997 at least 49 murders were committed by US fascists.

In India, the Bharatiya Janata Party (BJP) believes Hinduism is the true religion of India. It aims to force the country to accept Hindu laws, although 100 million Indians, 11 per cent of the population, are Muslim. In states where it has been elected, the BJP has scapegoated Muslims. In Bombay, Bangladeshi Muslims who have lived in India for years have been accused of taking jobs from Indians. The government has deported them back to Bangladesh. To try to 'persuade' them not to return, police officers have often beaten the men and raped the women.

◀ *Muslims who have tied a Hindu man to a handcart pulling him through the streets of Bombay, India during the 1992 riots. The riots started after extreme Hindus destroyed the Muslim Ayodhya mosque.*

7. What can we do?

How can people stop racism?

Throughout history, wherever there has been racism, there have always been people who have fought against it. Sometimes racist governments have been brought to their knees.

African-Americans did not get treated equally in the USA even after the ending of slavery in 1865. They were paid lower wages and had poorer homes and schools. In the 1960s many black and white people joined the civil rights movement. This massive campaign of meetings, marches and demonstrations forced the government to change the laws to make them fairer to black people. It did not solve all black people's problems but it was a big step in the right direction.

The Reverend Martin Luther King, one of the main leaders of the US civil rights movement. He is shown with leaders of the Civil Rights March from Selma to Montgomery, Alabama in 1965.

```
            FACT:
Montgomery, Alabama, 1955: Rosa
Parks, an African-American woman
  tired after her day's work, sat
down in the only remaining seat
 - in the whites-only part of the
bus. A white man demanded to sit
down but she refused to get up.
This sparked off the Montgomery
  bus boycott, and the start of
   the US civil rights movement.
```

One of the greatest recent struggles was the fight against apartheid in South Africa. In 1948, the South African government brought in the apartheid system. It divided its people into separate 'races', giving whites the most rights and black Africans the fewest. Black people could not mix with white people; they had separate schools, towns, buses – and even park benches. Most lived in poverty. The struggle against this unfair system included demonstrations, strikes and guerrilla war.

▲ *South African President Nelson Mandela in 1994 addressing a crowd at a meeting in memory of the student protests against apartheid in 1976. The banner shows Hector Peterson, a student who died in the protests.*

Many ordinary people from all around the world supported it. Apartheid was overthrown in the early 1990s when South Africa elected its first black president, Nelson Mandela.

In Australia, Aborigines have battled to win equal rights with the white population. In the 1960s, young Aborigines started their own civil rights movement. They took a new pride in their Aboriginal lifestyle and culture. Their main campaign was to win back the land that was taken from them during European settlement. Finally, in 1993, Prime Minister Paul Keating agreed with their claim and Aborigines began to recover land.

Organizing and protesting

If racists started to harass a family in your street, would you help to support that family? Stopping racism is not always a huge struggle against a political power like the apartheid government in South Africa. Often it's a matter of stopping a few thugs before they grow powerful.

Many people, both black and white, are horrified by racism and will take to the streets to protest against it. In Austria, large numbers of people were shocked when Jörg Haider, leader of the far-right Freedom Party, came second in the national elections of October 1999. The Freedom Party has its roots in the Austrian Nazi Party, which ruled the country during the Second World War. Austrians protested against Haider's party in their thousands. They feared that the success of this fascist organization would lead to growing racism in their country.

◀ A demonstration in Belgium following the election of Jörg Haider in Austria. The middle poster says 'Fascism never again' and calls for the stopping of Vlaams Blok, a Belgian far-right political party.

▼ *Rodney King who was brutally beaten by white policemen in Los Angeles, USA in 1992. The policemen weren't convicted, which sparked riots in the city.*

"
'You have to take a stand against racism.'
Regina Horst
'[I came] to make a symbolic gesture and try to give another picture of Germany.'
Flavia-Victoria Mai
Supporters of an anti-Nazi demonstration of about 200,000 people in Berlin, Germany, November 2000
"

An event that shocked British people was the murder of Afro-Caribbean teenager Stephen Lawrence in London, England in 1993. The police did not arrest the suspects, even though they had information about a gang of five racists who carried knives and boasted about using them on local black people.

Most Britons would not have heard of Stephen if it had not been for the courage and strength of his parents, Neville and Doreen. They kept pushing the police to find their son's killers. Ordinary people around the country supported their efforts. Five years later the government held an official inquiry, and admitted that there was institutional racism in the police force, which had not worked hard enough to find Stephen's killers.

How can we help?

If you hear racist remarks or jokes, or there is racist bullying at your school, you can try doing some or all of these things:

• Speak out. If you say nothing, others may think you agree
• Invite speakers from different communities to help to break down prejudice
• Organize discussions about human rights and racism
• Form a school policy against racism
• Join an anti-racist or human rights organization

Sport can be a great way of breaking down racism. In 1978, a national football competition was started in South Africa with mixed black and white teams. This meant that football was one of the first areas in which apartheid was ended.

▼ Ian Wright, football player for England.

> 'If I score goals, I'm English; if I demonstrate against racism, I'm a race relations problem, with a chip on my shoulder.'
> Ian Wright, English professional footballer

In many countries, such as Burundi in Central Africa and Colombia in South America, football is used as a way of bringing together communities that have been fighting.

It's up to all of us to do what we can. We would all be happier in a society free from the fear, distrust, ignorance and prejudice that cause racism.

▶ *Having friends from different cultures makes life richer and more interesting.*

case study · case study · case study · case study · case study

Mary Seacole Comprehensive Girls' School in the Midlands, England has students from many backgrounds. Just under half are from South Asian families, a third are white, and about 18 per cent are Afro-Caribbean. To tackle the problem of racism, the students were involved in making an anti-racist policy. Some of the teachers weren't keen at first, but the girls' enthusiasm persuaded them that change was needed.

Now, the students often deal with racist incidents themselves. As one girl says, 'We find if people are racist…that the person [making the comments] is isolated. You know, even their own friends will isolate that person.' Most of the white girls take the issue just as seriously. All the girls talk about the benefits of knowing people from different cultures and religions. They are more confident about questioning other things that go on in school, too.

GLOSSARY

Abused
Insulted or attacked.

Anti-Semitism
Hatred of Jewish people, which by the late nineteenth century had become a new kind of hatred based on ideas about 'race'.

Apartheid
'Apartness'. The apartheid system was brought in by the white South African government in 1948. It kept white, black and mixed race peoples separate and unequal.

Asylum
The right to live in another country if you are under attack in your own. People who suffer because of their skin colour, culture, religion or political beliefs often flee to other countries to try to claim this right. They are called asylum seekers.

Boycott
To get together with other people to refuse to have anything to do with a company, group of people, or foreign country.

British National Party (BNP)
A far-right political party in Britain, formed in the 1980s, which supports racial discrimination and is against immigration.

Civil rights
The rights of people in a country to live freely and equally, whatever their ethnic group or personal views.

Civil war
War between two or more groups of people within a country.

Colonialism
When one country rules another land as if it owned it.

Crack baby
A baby whose mother used the drug crack when she was pregnant. When the baby is born, it is addicted to the drug.

Deport
To send a person back to the country from which they came.

Discrimination
Treating a group of people worse than other groups.

Ethnic group
A group of people who share a common culture, tradition and perhaps language.

Ethnic minority
A group of people who have a different culture, religion, language or skin colour from most other people in their society.

European Union (EU)
An organization of western European countries that trade together and try to agree on certain common policies, for example, how they deal with asylum seekers.

Fascism
A extreme right-wing system of government based on the belief that one country or ethnic group is better than all others, and the need to obey one powerful leader.

Fascist
A person who believes that their country or ethnic group is better than all others, and obeys a powerful leader.

Genetics
The study of how physical features are passed on from parents to their offspring.

Ghettos
Parts of a city, especially very poor areas, where minority groups tend to live.

Guerrilla war
War fought by bands of fighters against a regular army.

Harass
To keep troubling and annoying someone.

Hispanics
Spanish-speaking people living in the USA, whose families come from Latin America.

Ignorant
Not knowing about a subject.

Immigrants
People who enter another country to live there.

Ku Klux Klan
An extreme right-wing secret society, founded in the southern states of the USA in the 1860s to oppose giving rights to black people. It still exists today. The KKK attacks Jews and non-white people.

Migration
The movement of people from one country to another.

Nazis
Supporters of Adolf Hitler's Nazi Party in Germany in the 1930s and 1940s.

Pensioners
People who no longer work and who receive money to live on, called a pension, usually from the government.

Primitive
Simple, undeveloped.

Raped
Forced to have sex.

Reservations
Areas, usually of poor land, where Native Americans were made to live after they were forced off their territories in the nineteenth century.

Stereotype
Something that is said about a whole group of people, such as 'All Jews are rich'. A stereotype is not based on fact and is insulting. It means people from that group are seen as all the same and not as individuals.

Vandalize
To damage or destroy buildings deliberately.

Xenophobia
Hatred of people from other countries.

FURTHER INFORMATION

ORGANIZATIONS

Australia and New Zealand
ACT Human Rights Office
3rd Floor GIO House
City Walk
Canberra ACT 2600
Australia

Citizens' Association for Racial
Equality (CARE)
PO Box 10.50.35
Auckland
New Zealand

Commonwealth Human Rights
Equal Opportunity Commission
GPO Box 5218
Sydney
NSW 2000
Australia

South Australian Equal
Opportunity Commission
GPO Box 464
Adelaide
SA 5001
Australia

Europe
SOS Racisme Internationale
64 Rue de la Folie Mericourt
Paris 75009
France
www.sos-racisme.org

UK
Commission for Racial Equality
Elliot House
10–12 Allington Street
London SE1E 5EH
Tel. 020 7828 7022
www.cre.gov.uk

Institute of Race Relations
2–6 Leeke Street
King's Cross Road
London WC1X 9HS
Tel. 020 7833 2010
www.irr.org.uk

Minority Rights Group
379 Brixton Road
London SW9 7DE
Tel. 020 7978 9498
www.minorityrights.org

Runnymede Trust
133 Aldersgate Street
London EC1A 4JA
Tel. 020 7600 9666
www.runnymedetrust.org

USA
International Organization for
the Study of Human Rights in
the United States
(EAFORD)
2025 Eye Street NW, Suite 1120
Washington DC 20006

Websites
http://saxakali.com
US site with material about
racism around the world.

www.antifa.net/yre/
Website of Youth against
Racism in Europe.

www.blink.org.uk
Black Information Link – for
Asian, African and Caribbean
community groups in the UK.

www.wiesenthal.com
Focuses on anti-Semitism
around the world.

BOOKS TO READ

How Racism came to Britain
(Institute of Race Relations,
1985)
Life Files: Racism by Jagdish
Gundara and Roger Hewitt
(Evans, 1999)
Prejudice and Difference by Paul
Wignall (Heinemann, 2000)
Racism, edited by Craig
Donellan (Independence
Educational Publishers, 1999)
*Racism: Changing Attitudes
1900–2000* by R. G. Grant
(Hodder Wayland, 1999)

For teachers:
*Jewish Perspectives on Racism: A
Primary School Resource* (Jewish
Council for Race Equality, 1998)
*Refugees – A Resource Book for
Primary Schools* by Jill Rutter
(Refugee Council, 1998)

Video
Show Racism The Red Card
(European Year Against Racism).
Video pack using famous
professional footballers as anti-
racist role models. Available
from Manchester Development
Education Project Ltd, c/o
Manchester Metropolitan
University, 80 Wilmslow Rd,
Manchester M20 2QR,
Tel. 0161 445 2495

INDEX